Only Beautiful Remains

Words of a Poet

Only Beautiful Remains

Words of a Poet

Written by Catherine Mellen

NFB
Buffalo, New York

Copyright © 2024 By Catherine Mellen

Printed in the United States of America

Only Beautiful Remains/ Mellen 1st Edition

ISBN: 978-1-953610-75-1

Poetry
Poetry> Female Author
Poetry> Survivor

No part of this book may be reproduced or transmitted in any form by any means, electronic or mechanical, including photocopying, recording, or by any information storage and retrieval system without permission in writing by the author.

NFB Publishing
119 Dorchester Road
Buffalo, New York 14213
For more information visit Nfbpublishing.com

This book is dedicated to the poets,
the lovers and the broken hearted.

The Poems

Chapter One: Faith

Once Occupied Chair	15
A Stairway	16
Thank You Jesus	17
Biggest Fear	18
Oh Starry Night	19
Eternity	20
A Day Trip	21
Once Upon A Staircase	22
Blue Moon	23
My Wishes	24
Circle of Life	25
Compass Star	26
Soulmates Through Life	27

Chapter Two: Life

Stranger's Hero	31
Decision's	32
Life	33
Dear Friend	34
Searching	35
Human Life	36
Tiny Tots	37
A Parent's Love	38
Yesterday's	39
Don't Run	40
Hopes	41
Best Friend	42

A Snowflake	43
Phone Time	44
Brand New Teardrop	45
Arrogant & Egotistic People	46
A Life Lived	47
Querying	48

Chapter Three: Love

Honest Eyes	53
Blue Bird Black Bird	54
Our Dream House	55
Never Let Go	56
Tender Hearts	57
Love	58
If Only	59
Time	60
Life's Gift	61
Feelings	62
One of a Kind	63
Special Someone	64
A Break-Up	65
A Goodbye	66
Lost Love	67
Wanted Confusion	68
A Broken Love Story	69
Faded Away	70
A Destined Wait	71
What You Hold	72
Many Ways Of Love	73

Chapter: Four Society

American Dream	77
New England	78
Lowell Spinners	79
Shattered Heart Pieces	80
Don't Drink and Drive	81
Punishment	82
Only One World	83
Change of Mind	84
Harmony	85
Beautiful World	86
Coronavirus	87

Chapter: Five Pieces of Me

Keeper Of My Heart	91
Cards I've Been Dealt	92
My Favorite Heartache	94
So Much More	96
Not A Clue	98
Just Words	99
No One Seems To Stay	100
My Bookshelf Heart	102
Do I Tell Him	104
Only Beautiful Remains	106
About the Author	109

Welcome to my book of poetry. A place where my words stumble upon stairs of faith, through the teardrops of life and the tender hearts of love, whilst the harmony of society sings and all the beautiful that remains in the tiny pieces of myself.

Chapter One

Faith

Hugs from heaven are the best to receive...
They are the ones that can not be deceived.

Once Occupied Chair

Creeping up behind me, I did not see you there
Sitting in the spot of your once occupied chair.
I left the seat empty, occupied only by you.
To keep in my memory, the love between us two.

Although I can't see you, I know you are here
I often feel your presence in your once occupied chair.
I am not the only to feel the love of a lost
Keeping the chair empty like a cold winter's frost.

Trying to reassure us they did not disappear
Keeping their memory going, in their once occupied chair.
Everyone has a lifetime with loved ones to share
Feeling the loss of a once occupied chair.

The memories are worth it, the tears come well due
No matter the empty chair, I'll keep looking for you.
Keep finding your way so I know you are near
I'll sit right beside, waiting at your once occupied chair.

A Stairway

Up to heaven's stairs an angel does wait...
Shining with happiness at the doors of heaven's gate.

Inside the angels blossom with glee...
Forever there is happiness throughout eternity.

Don't be afraid should your light shine...
Everyone becomes an angel one day in time.

The heart stops from all the aching and pain...
The soul lives on from all in life you gain.

So climb up those stairs. There's no need to hesitate...
There is so much happiness, once you're through heaven's gate.

Thank You Jesus

Help me Jesus, I'm writing a song
A music sheet where words belong.

There is no rush, take your time
Making our words into a rhyme.
Beautiful sounds for all to hear
Echoing in halls far and near.

Help me Jesus, it needs to be heard
Give peace a chance into a word.

A rhythm, a sound, a single prayer
Serenity in words for all to hear.
A hand, support, a strangers smile
Contagious with kindness in a single file.

Help me Jesus, the world seems so cold
So many promises are yet to be told.

Clean up the streets, rid the world of hate
For the children of tomorrow, it's not too late.
Give peace a chance and keep it going
Kindness and smiles will continue flowing.

Thank you Jesus, I know you can hear
Together we made this song into a prayer.

Biggest Fear

Dear God,

I know I have sinned, I'll prove to you I can do fine.
If only you'll give in and give me a little more time.

I know I did wrong when I told you I'd quit it all.
But I just kept going on, doing drugs and drinking alcohol.

I was young and thought it was cool. I thought it was fun and now I'm the fool.

I have so many friends who care, I have so much to give.
Death is my biggest fear, please Lord let me live?

I haven't got much time, they're taking me away.
Quick Lord make up your mind, they are burying me today.

My drug habit will be through, I promise I will go straight.
Lord don't take me with you, please don't say it's too late?

Everyone is grieving. I've hurt them can't you see?
Why are they leaving? Tell me what's to become of me?

I guess my life is at its end, you didn't answer my prayer.
Tell me Lord, what happens? Death is my biggest fear.

Oh Starry Night

Starry starry night,
I wonder if you can read my thoughts
My dreams, wishes and forget-me-nots.
Starry starry night,
Can you see the world below
The war, unjust and the secrets I know?

What do you think when you see the world
The love and hate combined and twirled?
Do you remember when the earth was new
Like a flower blooming in a springtime dew?
Can you see the love the world does hold
Written in hearts and wanting to be told?

Starry starry night,
I know you're always shining from above
Shimmering your light, your warmth and your love.
Starry starry night,
A darkened sky full of sparkle and shine
Giving way to beauty, love and all thing's fine.
A lovely dimension, no two are the same
Shining so brightly like an eternal flame.

Making wishes I often do
Praying for hopes to always come true.
Thank you for being such a delight
Glowing my darkness with your light.
Continue to turn my eyes so bright
A serenity of warmth feeling so right.
Oh starry night.

Eternity

Spirits fly throughout the air
As the earth spins around.
No one can see them here
No one can hear their sound.

They try to understand all of mankind
Whether it be love or evil on one's mind.
They don't judge, their flight is pure
Hoping to end evil and spread love forever more.

The spirits will fly all eternity through
And one day a spirit will be that of you.
Lives will go on, the earth will still spin
Your life on earth maybe gone,
But forever with spirits you will sing.

A Day Trip

If heaven wasn't so far away
I'd take a trip and visit for the day.

I'd visit my dad who left so long ago
Stop in on friends, just to say hello.

I'd spend time with Ma who left too soon
Hang out with Jon and dance by the moon.

I'd come back home and hug the ones I love
And tell them of my day with our loved ones above.

Make some plans for another day
If only heaven wasn't so far away.

Once Upon A Staircase

Once upon a staircase
A giant step I made
Looking up to struggles
Down a waterfall cascade.

Another step is taken
A giant leap I take
All the different stages
With every step I make.

Once upon a staircase
Another step I took
Growing through the pages
Of a written journal book.

Inked in footprints
Left behind by stain
If I keep going
Only a few steps remain.

Once upon a staircase
I looked up the last time
A cascade of courage
In taking the last climb.

I took the final steps
A fear I had to face
I finally got there
Once upon a staircase.

Blue Moon

October sadness
Bluest month of all.
Sky turns grey
Leaves start to fall.
The wind will howl
And chill fills the air.
Letting you know
Autumn weather is here.
Days will rise and nights will fall.
Shining its blue moon
For the saddest month of all.

My Wishes

There is a star way up in the sky
We got this far and it knows why.

I wished for your love
All my wishes have come true.

The star that stands so high above
Has given us love for me and you.

I make a wish on a silent thought
I wish the same as before.

I know I may wish a lot
But it helps us love each other even more.

So if you're ever lonely one night
Take a look up at a star.

It's the one that shines so bright
That got us this far.

Circle of Life

The wolf holds the heart, that we all feel
The tree is the soul, that makes our life real.

The bird carries the eyes, so we all can see
The beauty of life, that created you and me.

The moon, the stars and the clouds of stonish clay
They are the barriers that lead onto heavens way.

The wolf, the bird and of course the tree
Represents the heart whose eyes and soul go free.

My Compass Star

Another year passes and tears I shed
Remembering the words you once said
Broken heart pieces, stitched at the scar
Being held together by my compass star.

I know your looking down, guiding my way
I feel your presence like a warming sun ray
A comfort of knowing you're not that far
Walking beside me, my compass star.

You built my soul with your planted seeds
Sealing my scars from the burning bleeds
Never a doubt, though freaky and bizarre
Keeping me company, my compass star.

Said in a promise, you will never leave
Faith in my heart, I'll always believe
Up so high, standing where you are
Watching over me, my compass star.

Visions of you remain crystal clear
Never far away, you are always near
Memories I saved and put into a jar
Sacred and precious, my compass star.

Written in poetry and promises kept
Sealed in my heart and tears I wept
Darkened at night, shinning from afar
Always there for me, my compass star.

Soulmates Through Life

This is a story of a boy and a girl,
Placed on earth to live in this world.

Boy lives life doing the best he can
Growing from a boy, to becoming a man.
Girl lives life wanting all in the world
Becoming a woman, no longer a girl.

Older they grow, their eyes never greet
Soulmates they were, in heaven they will meet.
And laugh at the reason life passed them by
Too busy they lived, no time to even try.

Saw the two paths they were given to live
Had they slowed down with more time to give.
They'd see in life, their eyes did meet
Everyday they passed each other in the street.

Chapter Two

Life

Sometimes we have to be our own hero to become someone else's

A Strangers Hero

An act of terrorism
A foreign man's will
What he did the day
The world stood still.
No act of evil could ever compare
As we heard the news, terrorism was here.

The planes had crashed
So many lives lost
Their souls not forgotten
No matter the cost.
Strangers came together
And friendships were bound
Assuring families their loved ones would be found.

As days went by
It just got worse
But hearts of strangers
Was our only source.
Believing in faith and through God's will
We all came together, the day the world stood still.

Decisions

Everyday you take a chance
A chance you hope you don't regret.
And as you are taking the chance
You hope to get what you expect.

Everyday you make a choice
A choice you make on your own.
And you hope the choice you make
Makes your happiness be known.

Sometimes the chance you take
Leaves you unhappy and blue.
Or the choice you make
Really isn't the one for you.

Whether you win or lose
That's the chance you take.
You won't know the answer
Unless there's a choice to make.

The chances and choices
You do each and every day.
Are the lessons of life
You learn in your own unique way.

Life

Life has its ups and downs
It has it's turning twist.
There is sunshine and snowstorms
And also rain and mists.

Life can turn dark as black
Or bright and sunny with glee.
Life can feel like the end
But it can also feel like eternity.

Life is how you make it
Life is what you do.
You can't put life aside
It's something that comes with you.

Life can be a bit sane
It may have odds and ends.
But life wouldn't be easy
Without the life of a friend.

Dear Friend

Is there a friend
Who can lend an ear?
So when I need to talk
You will always be there.

Do you have a shoulder
One I can lean on?
For when I need some company
To sort out what is wrong.

Do you have a hand
One I can hold on to?
For when I need the strength
To help pull me through.

Do you have a heart
That is filled with love to share?
All I need is a true friend
Someone who really cares.

Are you that kind of friend, I have been looking for?
And if you are, *"Why haven't I met you before?"*

Searching

Through the woods I see a tree
In the sky there flies a bee.
On the ground I see some sand
At the beach, couples hand in hand.

Out all day I'll walk these streets
Out alone, looking for a friend to meet.
Different thoughts fill my mind
Looking for a friend and wasting my time.

Days went by, I walked many miles
Didn't get a hi not even a smile.
It seems so hard to find a friend
Another day, I wonder what will happen?

On and on I'll go my way
I will find a friend one of these days.
I know my search will have an end
When it does, I hope it's with a friend.

Human Life

Some people will remain in your life
And some will go away.
Some people you will forget about
And some, in memory will stay.

Some people will be just as friends
And others close at heart.
While others can be your enemies
And tear your world apart.

Some people can lie to your face
And some you can trust the best.
Some people will live through life
While others are laid to rest.

People may be just as they please
I know this sounds strange.
But a person's personality
Is something you can not change.

Tiny Tots

A little boy with a brand new toy.
His ripped up jeans and his boyhood dreams.
A little girl with thin hair and a tiny curl.
Holding her favorite doll, dreaming to grow beautiful and tall.

Both crying to get their way
Facing the world with each new day.
Then the school days come
And their tiny tot days are done.

You can't believe how fast they grew
They were just babies now their teenage years are through.
It makes you smile, yet there's a little frown
As you see your tiny tots in their graduation gown.

Growing up and growing old..
Seeing your little boy so big and bold.
Then as you turn around to see..
There's your little girl as beautiful as can be.

A Parent's Love

You give life to a child and you help them grow
Sometimes they'll need a hand for that push to go.

They'll need to hear words, those that say you care
So when they awake in the morning, they'll know you're there.

You give them directions to start out their day
To make sure they start it out in the right way.

And as they grow older, you see all they do is right
They may make mistakes, but they know day from night.

They know what to do from the words you say
The choices they make, are up to them on that day.

They got this far from the love they received from you
From your words of wisdom and everyday things you do.

And as they grow older, their life they will try to understand
But they'll know they got this far, from the help of a parent's hand.

Yesterday's

Yesterday is now gone
In your thoughts it still goes on.
You can not throw it out
It's a part of you, you know all about.

What the future holds
Will always be untold.
Look back on the past
The loves that went so fast.

The friends who cared
The good and bad times you shared.
Remember those hot summer nights
Staying out till it was morning light.

Don't forget those cold winter days
So much has changed since those yesterday's.

Don't Run

Runaway from your problems
They'll come back another day.
Runaway from all your heartache
They will find you some other way.

Runaway from a difficult encounter
They will run right back into you.
Runaway from an easy moment
They will wish you had stayed through.

Runaway from all you face
They will come back and make you blush.
Runaway from all in time
Just don't run away all that much.

Hopes

You hope your life is one you always desire
You hope your love is an endless flame of fire.
You hope your future is all your dreams come true
You hope your happiness is what you want to show of you.
You hope all your hopes, all come true your way
And if they don't, just keep hoping for another day.

Best Friend

I was a song still unsung
Like a little kid who has no fun.
I was a poem without a rhythm
Like a dancer that is out of line.
I was a voice without a tone
A piece of skin that is missing bone.
I was always one, no one to help me through
That all changed the day I met you.

A Snowflake

A wet beautiful snowflake
Glistening in its own lake.
Frozen in time, nowhere to go
Resting on a branch above the snow.
One of a kind, not like the others
Shining its beauty until it smothers.
A wet beautiful snowflake
Its beauty I got to partake.

Phone Time

Shattered screens
Put those phones down.
The dash that's in between
Is for the people you want around.
There's the day you were born
And the day that you die.
Don't waste your dash
On a shattered screen that makes you cry.

Brand New Teardrop

Brand new little teardrop running down my cheek
Sorry you must visit in my pains highest peak.
Although I feel a comfort that you would feel my pain
A tiny little teardrop, falling down like rain.

Back again my tiny teardrop, I'm sorry I'm not that strong
I'm glad you came to visit again, my strength it seems is gone.
I don't mean to be a bother or keep wasting your time
I'm glad you're here to support me when my pain is at its prime.

Tiny little teardrop why must you visit again
I'm trying to live without you, I don't want to be your friend.
I want my face to smile, I want my heart to feel good
I wish you would stay away, if only you could.

Tiny little teardrop you're like an old withered routine
Slicing through my happiness with your teardrops in between.
You've gotten kind of boring, an old habit to name a few
It's time for me to start over, making teardrops that are new.

Why must you return to my eyes that cry?
I've told you many times, it's time we say goodbye.
I wiped away your tears, their flow I did stop
I just didn't know each time, it was a brand new teardrop.

Arrogant & Egotistic People

Don't take for granted
The life you have here
Take a moment to breathe the fresh air.

Try all you can to taste
Spicy, sweet and sour
Take a moment to stop and smell a flower.

Don't wait for when
Only a memory to think of
To tell someone it is them you love.

Don't pass up a moment
To hold a loved one's hand
Or explain a situation if it's what you understand.

You could wake up one day
And it'll all be gone
Taken for granted, your life as you carried on.

A Life Lived

In the depths of life
The experiences you'll see
Reflects the emotions
Of what's meant to be.

The heart takes control
Of all those you'll love
The mind keeps you going
Guiding you through above.

Those precious moments
With loved ones around
Destined in your life
Your fate was bound.

In the depths of life
The experiences you'll see
Reflects the life
Of what was meant to be.

Querying

A querying I will go, a querying I will go
Emailed my submission, a querying I will go.
It started off real slow
First page was years ago
It's finally in completion and polished with a glow.

Pages I had to type, editing was the hype
My book is finally complete, my writing skills are ripe.
Some lines I had to wipe
I complained without a gripe
A rejection letter to delete and an agent I will swipe.

Proposal written well, a story I have to tell
I'll spread awareness, with words I often yell.
Querying can be hell
Making fingers swell
Guidelines are for fairness, an agents calling bell.

Proofread once again, spacing lines too thin
Hoping for a book show, a best seller for the win.
Attach files in trash bin
No writing with a pen
A querying I will go, until an agent says I'm in.

Chapter Three

Love

Poetry grew in her soul... With every breath, her words sliced beauty where only ugly once roamed.

Honest Eyes

I sat on your lap, your hand on my knee
You said, *"Look in my eyes as I count to three,*
Say what it is, that is on your mind..
If we say the same, we're definitely one of a kind."

We matched our words that we had said
We almost fell over as you bumped my head.
"How did we do that?" we questioned each other.
There's no way, that could be done by another.

Ya, it was freaky, but yet it was cool
Knowing neither of us, played the other a fool.
The feelings we had, we would always discuss
The talk that night, our eyes spoke of trust.

Forever goes the heart, forever goes the soul
Forever are the eyes of a love you don't let go.
"My future," are the words we both said
Keep it in the heart and it will never shed.

The feelings we'd say of what we both felt
Explain how it is, the way we make each other melt.
Forever are the words of our honest eyes
Forever for us, never a break up or goodbye.

Blue Bird Black Bird

Walking the streets
Through roads so narrow
Looking for a love
Like a blue jay and a sparrow.

How do I find or put into words
A love complete like a swarm of birds?
Resting on a wing, so much to discuss
The flight is pure, with a layer of trust.

Blue bird, black bird
Where you be?
Which one is you?
And which one is me?

Nesting down, a love anew
Serenity sounds of morning dew.
On the wire of flying herds
A love complete like a swarm of birds.

Walking the streets
Along the cupids arrow.
I finally found a love
Like a blue jay and a sparrow.

Our Dream House

We'll spread it with love
And go on from there
Build it with dignity
And a touch of loving care.

Frame it with friendship
So it is sturdy and strong
Cover it with trust
That will go on and on.

Heat it with our hearts
Together as one
Furnish it with care
The kind we have won.

Seal it with pride
One we have grown
And put it all together
In our home sweet home.

Never Let Go

A feeling came upon me
A feeling I can't help to show
A feeling that's inside of me,
One I'll never let go.

A feeling of love, a feeling of you
A feeling I love to feel,
Do you feel the same way too?

A feeling deeper than my heart
A feeling greater than my soul
A feeling that brought us together,
One I never want to let go.

A feeling that brightens my day
A feeling that adds light to my nights
A feeling that makes me scream,
I love you with all my might.

A feeling of your touch
A feeling that says yes instead of no
A feeling of loving each other,
One I never want to let go.

Tender Hearts

You tell me you still love me
You miss me very much
How often you long to hold me
Feel my kiss and my touch.

You say you weren't happy
During the time we spent apart
You want to be together again
And make a fresh new start.

My head is telling me not to
You will hurt me once again
My heart is saying I need you
Just name the time and when.

I know I'll come back to you
I need to have you near
I'm placing my heart into your hands
Please handle it with tender care.

Love

Today is here, yesterday is gone
But the love from then, still grows strong.
Come tomorrow, as the days will pass
I'm glad to say our love will last.

What we have is a dream come true
My dream was completed when I met you.
I never thought love was real
But when you're in love, it's all you feel.

Never a day, I'd be on my own
And never a night I'd spend all alone.
I know for a fact you'll always be there
And if you can't be, your heart will be near.

You must know I'll always be by your side
Your love has given me so much pride.
Forever is what our love will be
I must say, *"I love you honestly."*

If Only

If I was the wind and you the rain
We would mix together, only love without pain.
Only happiness is what we would share
And everyone would see how much we really care.
There would be no writing, only words to say
Never a miss you, only together we'd be everyday.

Time

Time can stand still, time can go on.
Time can go away and time can be gone.
Time can be left for memories, it can also be left to forget.
But the times I spend with you, are the ones I'll never regret.
Time can go fast, time can go slow
The times we are together, are ones I'll never let go.
Time can end so suddenly, time can end so fast
If our time was to end, I'll never forget our time in the past.

Life's Gift

The love of a soul is yet to be mine.
This love I'll receive in the future of time.
It'll be my key to the happiness ahead
There in the morning and at night while I rest in bed.
Of course they'll be another who will help build this soul
Together we'll be a family, not half but as a whole.
The love of this soul will be forever and true
As we raise this love, together me and you.

Feelings

There's a certain kind of feeling
That is floating in the air
A certain kind of feeling
That brings two people near.
It's a feeling that is hard to express
And you take the chances on what to expect.
It's a feeling that makes your heart skip a beat
It's a feeling that makes you tingle head to feet.
 It's a feeling, one you always dreamed of
    It's a feeling, the feeling of love.

One Of A Kind

Always on my mind
Are memories shared with you.
You are always there for me
Always pulling me through.

People say love matures over a long long time
From the very start it seems, our love is one of a kind.

A dream come true is a dream of you
You keep my spirits high.
I hope your feelings are just as strong
So our love will never die.

I feel your absence when we are apart
A feeling I can't help to show.
This love we share is so good
So rare, I'll never let it go.

This seems to be the perfect love
A love so hard to find.
In my heart I'll always know
Our love is one of a kind.

Someone Special

I look in the mirror and see in my eyes a special someone
And it comes as no surprise to know you are the one.

You fulfill my nights with a feeling that is rare
The way you hold me tight, I know you still do care.

You brighten my days when we spend them together
There are so many ways to say how we feel for each other.

When we are making love, the feeling I feel inside
You're all I ever dreamed of, my love I will not hide.

And when we go out whether there is something to do
There's so much to talk about as long as I'm with you.

>   I need you more in so many ways
>   My heart is what you have won.
>   I look forward to my nights and days
>   When they are shared with you,
>   My Special Someone.

A Break Up

I remember your warm embrace
The feeling of your touch.
I remember the smile on your face
And wanting you so much.

I remember being in your arms
We'd share each other's love.
You were my good luck charm
Everything I had dreamed of.

I was with you and you with me
Everything we had shared.
You had end so suddenly
As if you never even cared.

You left me with so much pain
And memories filled with sorrow.
You turned my sunshine into rain
With our shattered dreams of tomorrow.

A Goodbye

The love we shared
 I will never regret
How much you cared
I will never forget.

The relationship we had
Meant so much to me
And it makes me mad
It ended so suddenly.

I didn't want it to die
I wanted us to go on
You said goodbye
And within a minute you were gone.

This came as such a surprise
It's everything I feared
The look in your eyes
They didn't show a care.

Love works in many ways
I now know we are through
I'll always remember the days
When you loved me and I loved you.

Lost Love

When you have a love
You think will always last
Don't follow your heart
Because the love will end so fast.

It's not a game on whether you win or lose
It's not a bargain on which you pick or choose.

It's not a fling
Or a one night affair
Or the next morning
And you're not there.

It's not the thought of not knowing what to do
It's not wondering if the one you love, loves you.

It is the fact of knowing
What's going on
Then you wonder
Were you in the wrong?

It's always remembering a love that was so true
It's the lost love, that left you so blue.

Wanted Confusion

I don't want a commitment
Only one that is true.
Do as you please
Just keep me with you.

I want to know I'm the one,
You think so fond of
You're glad you found me,
Glad I'm the one you love.

We can trust each other
There's no need to lie.
And when we're not together
There will be nothing to hide.

If that isn't what you want
And you don't feel the same as me
Then all I can say
Is I am setting you free.

A Broken Love Story

For a while, I had you in the palm of my hand
For a while, I guess I couldn't understand.

I took it all for granted
And walked all over you.
Knowing you could leave me
But never thinking it to be true.
Taking away a memory
I knew your love was real.
Leaving you to unchain me
With the way I made you feel.

Was it words, I never tried to say?
Or was it anger, that made you go away?
For a while, I held you close to me
For a while, I knew we were meant to be.

Destined to meet, brought together by fate
I took advantage and turned my love into hate.
Seeing no reason to change my ways
Taking away the shine on your sunny days.

I caused you to walk and you found someone new
But for a while, in my hand, I held you.

Faded Away

It's been so long, it's hard to say
Of days so true, but yet faded away.

The visions are still so very clear
Everyday I am wishing you were here
Days go by, the pain lingers on
Wishing back for days already gone.

It's been so long, it's hard to say
I am missing you every single day
Forever the memories, I'll never let go
Feeling your love in my body, heart and soul.

Wishing for days of memories so true
Remembering the times once spent with you
Forever in memory, forever to hold
Sometimes in words that want to be told.

It's been so long, it's hard to say
Of days so true, but yet faded away.

A Destined Wait

You waited for me, a true caring man
Wanting to give, all that you can.
Strangers we were, destined to meet
Feelings of butterflies from head to feet.

You waited for me, you knew I would arrive
A long lasting love, destined to survive.
Hold me more with each passing day
Forever a promise, together we'll stay.

You waited for me, a moment you knew
I would be here, also waiting for you.
The moment I'm awake until I sleep
The love from your heart, I will always keep.

I waited for you while you waited for me
I knew one day, our love would be.
Honest, kind, loving and true
Lasting for all eternity through.

Here I am, standing by your side
In this path, together we will ride.
Forever and a day, my heart you have won
I'm so glad you waited, ever since day one.

What You Hold

The heart can hold, a many of things;
A soulmate, a love, family or friends
Laughter, joy, sadness and pain
Sometimes, it makes your mind go insane.

Don't follow your heart, always go with your mind
Should your heart be hit with a blow from behind.
The heart can take so much pain
That much is true.
The mind can make you happy
By forgetting the pain in you.
Don't forget the happy times
Or the loves you hold dear
The mind and heart go with you everywhere.

Try to do without pain, it can out do the heart
Though some is expected right from the start.
Just keep your mind clear
Though the heart may ache
Remember the mind is always
The first choice to make.
The mind wants to be happy
The heart can make you cry.
Just remember to stay positive
No matter how hard you try.

Many Ways Of Love

Love can be...
Soft and sweet as a gentle touch
Or words that hurt way too much.

Love can be...
Wrapped around your arms, warm and true
Or scared away when anger is raised to you.

Love can be...
Amazing and real without a doubt
Or always wondering what all the anger is about.

Love can be...
Unconditional, explained and listened well
Or unrespected and controlled by words that yell.

Love can be...
Filled with happy memories and happy days
It all depends on your love of many ways,

CHAPTER FOUR

Society

Poetry, because life is too hard to explain

American Dream

Struggling to make ends meet, happens on every street
Barely enough to get by, unpaid bills and funds run dry.

American dream, where did it go?
Was it a lie for the world to know?
Stress piles high, demand is too much.
The American dream I just can't touch.
Rent is due, kids need clothes
Shopping for bargains is how it goes.
American dream is what I was told
But rarely do I see it, actually unfold.

Homeless and mental health
Security from the commonwealth
Jobless rate and disability
A loss beyond our ability.
I look out the window of the American dream
Thinking it was a lie or so it does seem.
American dream where are you now?
Were you a lie we all believed in some how?

I'll close my eyes and dream of my home
An American myth I ponder alone.

New England

Watching petals bloom in full
Such a summer's sight.
Catching leaves fall from branch
An autumn's ray of light.
Icy roads without a choice
Is winter's frozen right.
Now the petals start to bloom
Spring time warmth in flight.

It's New England, what can I say?
Don't like the weather, just wait a day.

Four seasons in a week
Leaf changing colors at its peak.
Hot, warm, cold to the bone
It's a New England kind of home.

Lowell Spinners

The name of the team
Is what it's all about
Batters, pitchers, catchers
You'll find in the dugout.

Fans are waiting
For the throw of the first ball
Knowing the team
Gives each game their all.

Whether it be a strike, an out, a foul or a run
The game is baseball and it's always so much fun.

So grab a ticket, get your seat
And enjoy the game
Each game you go to
Is never the same.

The team may lose
Or come out as winners
It's always worth it
To watch the Lowell Spinners.

Shattered Heart Pieces

I carry the weight of a shattered heart
Society said, *"Move On"* So I played the part.
Accepting the way of my situation
Scattered emotions in duration.
Busting in words afraid to speak
An eagle's soar, like the courage I seek.

Way above the mountain, as high as they come
Shattered heart pieces in earths mighty kingdom.
Where do they go, tiny pieces of pain?
Where do they stay, if they must remain?

I carried the weight of a shattered heart
Reality said, *"Stay Strong"* So I played the part.
Accepting support as a donation
Scattered emotions and explanation.
Speaking my truth so I am heard
An eagle's soar with each new word.

Way above the mountain, as high as they come
Shattered heart pieces in earths mighty kingdom.
Where do they go, tiny pieces of my heart?
Where do they stay, if we never do part?

Don't Drink And Drive

I was only nineteen with a life still ahead of me,
I had one more beer and my life ended instantly.

They told me not to drive, but what did I do?
I didn't listen and now their hearts are in two.

I was only having a good time, a little fun now and then
I had too much fun and now my life is at an end.

I wish I could go back and put that beer back down
I'm laying in this casket feeling like such a clown.

Family and friends are all around me with a tear in each eye
Saying I was too young, much too young to die.

I guess I'm gone now, I won't live another day
But there's one last thing I'd really like to say...

"Let this be a lesson for all to survive,
Do me a favor and Don't Drink And Drive."

Punishment

You take a life without a thought in mind
Of all the loved ones, that are now left behind.

A life was cut short
By your own hands
With your own reasons
Only you can understand.

You did what you wanted, your mind was set
You plead, *"Not Guilty"* without a regret.

You're sent away for years
Only to be set free
To live a daily life
With others in society.

There are still loved ones who cry everyday
For that life you had taken away.

You live your life with no guilt, only pride
But when life is done, there's nowhere to hide.

The good get rewarded
As the bad does too
It always ends,
You get what was given from you.

Only One World

Why did it come to so much disgrace?
Why did we tear up the human race?
Why must a black man live a life in fear?
Why do people stand by without a care?

It's only one world, which we all must share
For every child, a right to live without living in fear.
It doesn't matter the color, for which you hold
Nor matters the religion, for which you are told.
We are all given one body, for which we must live
Equal is the reasoning, for which we must give.
It's only one world, which we all must share
Equal with love, for there is no compare.

Why did it come to so much hate?
Why did we let it continue to circulate?
It's time it stops, let's put an end to this fight
This land belongs to all, black, brown, not just the white.
Why must it come to so many deaths?
Why did America witness a man's last breath?
It's been too long, a change needs to come soon
No matter our color, we all sleep under the same moon.

Change of Mind

A change of mind
Can be a game of the heart.
A change of time
Can turn your world apart.

You think you have everything
In the palm of your hands.
Then a change just happens
And you don't understand.

You say your love will last endlessly
And you say the same for tomorrow.
Then a change comes so suddenly
And all you have left is sorrow.

There is no way to avoid a change
It happens all the time.
The feeling is so strange
It's a game in your mind.

So when a change comes your way
And you don't know what to do
Just remember everyday
There's a better change for me and you.

Harmony

Harmony,
It's what this world needs
Harmony,
In a broken world that bleeds.
Harmony, let's give it a chance
Stop this opinionated circumstance.

We are all fighting so many wars
Climbing mountains and swimming shores.
When does it stop for you and I?
When do we give harmony a try?

Sing a happy song,
Bring a smile upon your face.
Keep strumming along
Harmony will squeeze into place.

Dance to the beat
Listen to the sound
Tapping at your feet
Harmony is all around

Give a chance at peace
End all war and put evil at cease
Where does it begin for you and I?
Let the music in, give harmony a try.

Harmony,
Give music a chance
Join in on the dance
Harmony,
Like watered garden seeds
Harmony,
It's what the world needs.

Beautiful World

Blessed are the birds, lucky to fly so high
The eagles that soar, a cardinal gliding by
A blue jays whistle, the seagulls that steal
A woodpecker's peck or a hawk resting on a rail.

Lucky are the animals, blessed to roam free
The buffalo, zebra, elephant and the monkey
A lone wolf's howl, a hyena's laugh, a lion's roar
A bear who dances or the hippos who always snore.

Blessed are the lucky, the ones able to see
All this beautiful world has to offer you and me
The oceans so wide, a forever land of sea
This earth of ours, created for you and me.

Drugs are an epidemic and an everyday news brief
Laws made to abide, instead only cause grief
And being offended, it happens on every street
A new way of being with every person you meet.

Clean up our land, like in the older days
Everyone is so caught up, living life in their fast ways.

America the beautiful, let's keep it that way
Stand as a nation, respect our flag and kneel when you pray.

Coronavirus

Wear your mask, don't take it off
Is it a fever or just a cough?
Social distancing, practice it often
A new way of life, so easily forgotten.

Don't touch this, don't touch that
Wear gloves to avoid contact.
Coronavirus put the world at a stall
Cutting hours at stores and the mall.

Give a smile, no one can see
Stand in line, but not too closely.
Polish, shine and crystal clear
Cleaning products quickly disappear.

Stay safe, warm and healthy too
This is my wish for all of you.
Show me love from your mask
It's easy to do, just multi task.

Chapter Five

Pieces of Me

A broken shattered heart can still once again love, and yet, break once again still.

Keeper of My Heart

The keeper of my heart
Someone I once knew
Tucked securely inside
With no trace of a clue.

A friendship created
With smiles and laughter
Blanketed in silence
For many years after.

I was told to move on
Go out and date others
Like a blanket on a fire
The flame only smothers.

Superficial wounds
Never run that deep
With words entwined
Of these feelings I keep.

Encrypted in truth
A broken hearts code
Sealed in with desire
And the urge to explode.

A picture perfect frame
Hides the truth I speak
Mirrored over the image
Of loves highest peak.

The emptiness lingers
And plays a big part
Of how much I miss
The keeper of my heart.

Cards I've Been Dealt

It started so young
What else could I do
Spending my days
Just surviving through.

My first shuffle of tears
Blanketed my emotions
Pallets of burning stains
A stand-still of motions.

Unanswered questions
And the feelings I felt
Not really knowing
The cards I've been dealt.

My next round of tears
Was when I was older
A bitter winters draft
As emptiness grows colder.

A diamond, a spade
The clubs and the heart
The cards in my life
Have sure played their part.

A swelling of the eyes
The waves crashing in
Reminiscing the days
Of happiness within.

A stinging sensation
An unrequited pain
A waterfall of memories
Falling down like rain.

I find the positive
In all my heartaches
It keeps me smiling
While my heart breaks.

No matter the pain
Throughout the years
The cards I've been dealt
Fall from my tears.

My Favorite Heartache

You were the needle
And I was the thread
Stitched up the pieces
I once considered dead.

A tingling sensation
That started at my toes
Twinkled with sparkles
Straight up to my nose.

A quite charming man
Who wiped away my tears
Turned my words into poetry
And chased away my fears.

Crumbling the walls
I had built from trust
What was once a barrier
Became particles of dust.

Drowned in the empathy
With your caring ways
You added the sunshine
To my rain soaked days.

You came into my life
And I was never the same
The cards I've been dealt
And a cruel dating game.

One day you were there
And the next you were gone
Like seeds to a garden
Where no flowers stay long.

I'll dig up our memories
Every once in a while
When my days get rough
And I need myself a smile.

Remembering the pain
A bad habit I try to break
But my memory of you
Is my favorite heartache.

So Much More

I looked in his eyes
And the things I saw
Exploding emotions
So precious and raw.

I didn't know I'd fall
It caught me off guard
I tried to ignore it
But it was just too hard.

How could I have known
It would happen to me?
I should have seen
There was a possibility.

I didn't know
That my heart could
Or even it would
Or why it should.

A one sided love
It happens to a few
Born with experience
It's all I ever knew.

The questions linger
Answering is tough
Relationship material
Why am I not enough?

Touching my soul
Like sounds of a song
Harmony so perfect
Where did it go wrong?

This is my love story
Where did it begin?
He was so much more
But I was just a fling.

Not A Clue

I walked away, the very day
Our friendship had ended.
I didn't know, how it would go
I guess I just pretended.

He turned my days into warming rays
His friendship was so true.
The wandering eyes were no surprise
I just wish I never knew.

I didn't belong, so I moved along
To forget him the best I could.
Emotions tired, a heart rewired
Letting go, I knew I should.

I played the part of an unbroken heart
So no one would ever know.
Years gone by, I don't know why
My heart just won't let go.

Memories kept, tears I have wept
For a guy I meant nothing too.
The feel of his touch, I miss it so much
And he has not a clue.

Just Words

Just words... written on a wall
I gave my best, I gave my all.
Just words written, so easy to some
Butterfly flutters as memories come.
Just words written, with no voice
A friendship missed without a choice.
Just words written, I tried my best
Blending in, my heart needs a rest.
No words written, no number to call
I just miss him... written on my wall.

No One Seems To Stay

Her collection began quite young
Of her loves along the way
Never really knowing
Why no one seems to stay.

It started with her family
Though most she barely knew
She tucked them in her heart
Despite what she'd been through.

Sometimes she would question
What she did that was so wrong
It was hard understanding
Being part of a family you don't belong.

Her questions went unanswered
And remain to this very day
Still, she often wonders
Why no one seems to stay.

She formed a lot of friendships
Many which she holds dear
Some lasting a lifetime
While some would just disappear.

She remembers those who cared
And those who made her smile
Happy scattered memories
She's collected all the while.

Often they remind her
Of cards she's dealt to play
Just another scenario
Why no one seems to stay.

A few went off to Heaven
And they play a big part
Of the huge pile of love
She has resting in her heart.

Though heartaches often came
She found the positive in each
Blessed for the experience
And the lessons they did teach.

She keeps her collection close
In the hopes that some day
One may love her just enough
To make them want to stay.

My Bookshelf Heart

Her heart is a bookcase
Filled with books to read
Some are written with love
While others still do bleed.

Pages filled with her poetry
Written in blood, sweat and tears
You can almost feel her words
And some of her darkest fears.

Some are inked in footprints
While some leave behind a stain
Telling about her struggles
And her excruciating pain.

One tells of a friendship
Through tears she often wept
Giving a reason to believe
In a promise that was kept.

There's pages for the guy
Who broke her heart in two
And how she holds it together
With her paper and some glue.

Each person has a line
And some even a chapter
Her favorite books of all
Are the ones filled with laughter.

Some books she'll never read
And leave them to collect dust
For they are written words
Of the names she can not trust.

She holds her books tightly
Like those she loves the most
For each book on this shelf
Was written by the host.

Do I Tell Him

Do I tell him,
The truth I feel
Comfort in knowing
A friendship is real.

Do I tell him,
The warmth I felt
In his arms
I'd so easily melt.

Would my words
Even matter at all
Tripped my emotions
I stumble and fall.

Do I tell him,
He's still the part
Tightly wrapped
Tucked in my heart.

Do I tell him,
I long for his touch
Or the simple fact
I miss him so much.

Butterfly flutters
Trembling scared
What if my words
Are all he had feared.

Do I tell him,
He's still on my mind
A friendship like ours
Not too easy to find.

Do I tell him,
Or not say a word
Rumors do spread
And maybe he heard.

Sacred little memories
I filled to the rim
Written in words
Afraid to tell him.

Only Beautiful Remains

The pieces of a broken heart
Are thick shards of glass
Each holding the memory
Of a time that has since pass.

A few carry the laughter
That life sometimes brings
A smile, a chuckle, a hug
And a million little other things.

Some carry an aroma
Of beautiful scented flowers
Reminders of the serenity
Captivated solace in the hours.

The hurt is buried deep
The weight of its pile gains
Inside its rigid pieces
Is where only beautiful remains.

There's a piece full of love
And pieces that carry joy
There's one always hidden
For it's a broken hearts decoy.

One piece is full of hope
Like a well-wishes dream
Collecting the teardrops
When things aren't what they seem.

Inside each of these pieces
Implanted perfect scenes
Shadowing around the hurt
Carving through the in-betweens.

Through all of life's obstacles
And its heartbreaking pains
The pieces of a broken heart
Is where only beautiful remains.

About the Author

Catherine is an American Poet, Author and Blogger. Born in 1969 Lowell, Massachusetts. She shares her story of horrific childhood trauma and the courage to shatter her silence on family secrets through her words of poetry and decade's of writing in journals. In 2015 she was disabled from injuries she suffered in an auto accident. Resulting in a permanent disability, horrifying repressed memories and a lot of free time to put over three decades of writing into multiple books.

Author of **Christmas in Poetry Land:** A delightful collection of Christmas Poetry. **Survivor's Mind**: A deep and dark poetic look into the world of childhood trauma, family secrets and inside the mind of a survivor. **A Childhood Tragedy Under A Mother's Watch: Part One 1975-1982 Lowell Massachusetts** and **A Life Given To Me: Part Two 1982-2019** where she shatters her silence on her childhood trauma, family secrets and the monstrous predator her birth mother harbored. **Understanding Childhood Trauma**: An informative book to help medical professionals, family, friends and society to better address victims of childhood trauma and family secrets.
She looks forward to sharing more of her poetry, memoir and fiction works. Follow Catherine on the Amazon and Goodreads app for updates of future publications.

Next Release, **A Promise Made, A Promise Kept:** A fascinating true story of friendship, faith and the unexplainable gift of a promise. Coming in Autumn 2024.

This collection of poetry began back in 1984 when words and poetry became the two things I could always count on. Even when pen and paper were unavailable to me, I was still able to put situations, friendships, relationships and faith into poetry. I hope these poems have touched your soul, warmed your heart, made you smile and most of all, I hope you have enjoyed reading Only Beautiful Remains.

www.ingramcontent.com/pod-product-compliance
Lightning Source LLC
Chambersburg PA
CBHW060819050426
42449CB00008B/1738